Pointing at the Wind

The Weather-Vane Collection of the Canadian Museum of Civilization

Pierre Crépeau

with the assistance of
Pauline Portelance

Canadian Museum of Civilization

Canadian Cataloguing in Publication Data

Crépeau, Pierre, 1927–

Pointing at the wind: the weather-vane collection of the
Canadian Museum of Civilization
Issued also in French under title, Signes des vents.

ISBN 0-660-12904-3
DSS cat. no. NM98-3/68-1990E

1. Weather vanes — Canada — History — Exhibitions.
2. Folk art — Canada — Exhibitions.
I. Portelance, Pauline.
II. Canadian Museum of Civilization.
III. Title.
IV. Title: The weather-vane collection of the Canadian
Museum of Civilization.

NK 9585.C73 1990   745.593   C90-098712-X

Printed in Canada

Published by
Canadian Museum of Civilization
100 Laurier Street
P.O. Box 3100, Station B
Hull, Quebec
J8X 4H2

Cover photo by Harry Foster

Contents

Acknowledgements

Our thanks to Canadian Centre for Folk Culture Studies (CCFCS) registrars John Corneil and George Barnhill, for their patience and determination in helping us locate the weather vanes in our collections. Thanks also to James Donnelly from History Division for his willing and cheerful assistance. The CCFCS cataloguers, Monique Morrissette and Barbara Dexter, provided expert assistance in retrieving files and documentation on the weather vanes.

The efficient work of Sylvie Régimbal and Nancy Struthers, of the Museum Library, enabled us to trace obscure publications. A special thank you to Dennis Fletcher, who gave generously of his time and talent to photograph most of the objects. The text was edited by Catherine Cunningham-Huston. Deborah Brownrigg was graphic designer and production officer; Francine Boucher prepared the camera-ready.

Introduction

Forecasting the Weather by Knowing the Wind Direction

Francis Bacon said: "Every wind has its weather." Since the dawn of history, hunters, sailors and farmers have scanned the skies before tracking their prey, launching their boats or sowing their fields. For those whose daily activities are determined by weather conditions and whose livelihood is subject to the whims of nature, weather forecasting is essential.

In the colonial era, abrupt changes in temperature and the inability to forecast the weather made farming particularly arduous for the first pioneers. Canada's climate is highly variable and unpredictable, with rapid drops in temperature, sudden torrential rains, unexpected treacherous storms and vastly different regional conditions. It is thus not surprising that the Canadian settler amassed a wealth of observations and developed meteorological knowledge based on weather signs. This purely empirical knowledge was the result of long experience acquired over the course of several generations. At one time or another, most of us have heard some old farmer, sniffing the wind and scanning the horizon, declare in a sententious tone and with as much authority as any full-fledged meteorologist: "It's going to rain tomorrow — the wind is blowing from the southeast."

This folk knowledge of the weather is often expressed in short rhymes referring to a variety of natural elements and phenomena: stars, clouds, fog, dew, rainbows, plants, seasons and animal behaviour. Here are some well-known examples:

If the moon rises pale, expect rain;
If it rises clear, expect fair.

Fog in the morning,
Sailor take warning;
Fog in the night,
Sailor's delight.

Rainbow in the morning,
Shepherd take warning;
Rainbow toward night,
Shepherd's delight.

When the dew is on the grass,
Rain will never come to pass;
When grass is dry at morning light,
Look for rain before the night.

Evening red and morning grey
Sets the traveller on his way;
Evening grey and morning red
Brings down rain upon his head.

When the wind is in the east
'Tis neither good for man nor beast.

A veering wind will clear the sky;
A backing wind says storms are nigh.

Winds that swing against the sun,
And winds that bring the rain are one.
Winds that swing round with the sun,
Keep the rain storm on the run.

If the wind back against the sun,
Trust it not for back it will run.

A weathercock that swings to the west
Proclaims the weather to be the best.
Weathercock that swings to the east
Proclaims no good to man or beast.

While each region has its own signs, wind direction is a universal indicator of weather, less by the direction in which it blows than by changes in direction and especially by the direction it is likely to take. A wind shifting from west to east is a sign of bad weather, whereas a wind heading from east to west heralds good weather. A flexible and accurate gauge of wind direction, the weather vane soon became an indispensable tool to the pioneer.

The Weather Vane through the Ages

The custom of erecting weather vanes on public and private buildings probably grew out of ancient rituals associated with the completion of construction work. Traditionally, rooftops were decorated with finials to celebrate the completion of a job and to appeal to benevolent spirits for protection (Fig.1).*
This ancient custom was carried on until fairly recently. After a barn-raising in Quebec, the most agile carpenter would place a bouquet of fir branches on the roof of the new building, thereby signalling the start of celebrations. In some communities, the finial received a blessing to protect the new building against lightning.

The invention of the weather vane was probably prompted by a wish to gauge wind direction so that the weather could be forecast. The earliest weather vanes consisted of strips of light cloth that were fastened to a vertical shaft and fluttered in the slightest breeze. However, as these streamers were not very

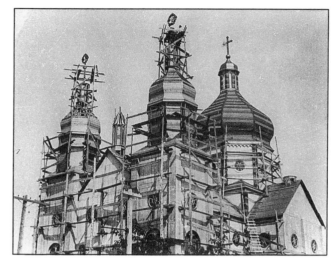

Figure 1. Construction of the Ukrainian Catholic Church of the Assumption of the Blessed Virgin Mary, Portage la Prairie, Manitoba, circa 1936. Note the wreath-shaped finials on the crosses atop the cupolas.

durable, they were eventually replaced by small boards made of light wood; mounted on spindles, these boards turned in the wind, showing its direction. Weather vanes were later fashioned of other materials such as iron and more malleable metals. In widespread use in the Western world, the weather vane has assumed a number of forms through the ages and has served a variety of social and cultural purposes.

The weather vane, as we know it today, dates back to the first century b.c., when the Greek astronomer Andronikos of Cyrrhos built the hydraulic clock in Athens — the "Tower of the Winds", also known in the Middle Ages as the "Lantern of Demosthenes". The tower is octagonal, each side featuring a carving of one of the eight major winds. On the peak, a bronze

---

*The abbreviation "Fig." refers to an illustration; "No." to an object in the collection.

Figure 2. Tower of the Winds, Athens.

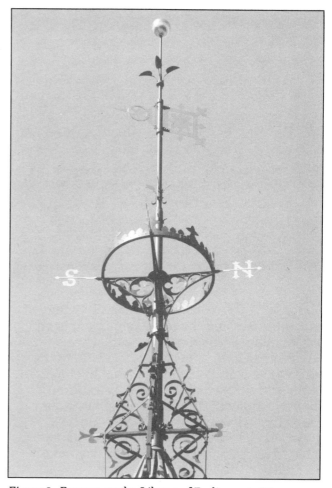

Figure 3. Pennon on the Library of Parliament, Ottawa.

Triton holding a rod turned with the wind, indicating its direction (Fig.2). This Triton is considered to be the earliest weather vane.

Another type of weather vane probably originated with the feudal ensign. In the Middle Ages, a feudal lord would attach a sheet of metal shaped like his coat of arms to a vertical shaft and hoist it onto the highest turret of his castle. However, the metal banner (or pennon) would often be toppled by strong winds. To avoid this, the banners were eventually mounted on spindles, allowing them to turn with the wind, and thus did double duty as weather vanes (Fig. 3 and No. 55).

Further north, Viking navigators mounted splendid bronze weather vanes on the bow or stern of their ships to indicate both direction and wind speed (Fig. 4).

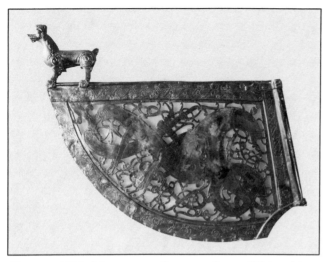

Figure 4. Gilded-bronze weather vane from a Viking ship.

Later, with the development and diversification of trades and the remarkable expansion of commerce, personalized weather-vane signs made their appearance. They filled the sky with a panoply of images evoking the daily activities of labourers. This tradition lives on today in the form of weather vanes depicting artisans and merchants. Horses, cows and fish are the most popular motifs, next to roosters, in Canadian weather vanes. In addition to gauging the weather, these weather vanes advertise the householder's occupation (Fig. 5 and 6; Nos. 32 and 48). The custom of adding the cardinal points under the main motif dates back to the mid-seventeenth century.

The art of the weather vane did not escape industrialization. Toward the mid-nineteenth century, machines took over the job of craftsmen; anonymous mass production supplanted personalized creations; and mail orders replaced the warm contact between craftsman and client (Figs. 7 and 8).

Figure 5. Goose made by Jennifer Connolly and mounted on top of her workshop, Almonte, Ontario.

How Weather Vanes Are Made

There are three basic techniques used by artisans to make weather vanes: cutting, carving and hammering.

Cutting is undoubtedly the simplest technique. The artisan cuts the desired motif — for example, a rooster, fish or horse — from a flat piece of wood or metal and mounts it on

Figure 6. Goose and tree on the gable of the barn of Knockeen farm, Hull, Quebec.

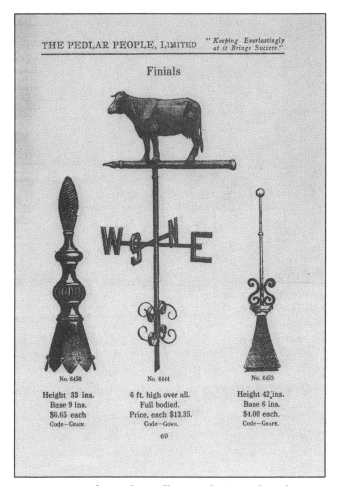

Figure 7. Page from *The Pedlar People Limited* catalogue, Oshawa, Ontario, 1912.

a spindle. The wood is usually cut with a coping saw, and rough edges are occasionally touched up with a penknife. Copper, tin and thin sheet metal are cut with shears. A hacksaw or blowtorch is used for plate or resistant metals. The cutting technique produces powerful, highly stylized designs, which are strikingly silhouetted against the sky. This no-fuss method focuses on achieving bold and dynamic lines (Nos. 2 and 88).

Although more difficult than cutting, wood carving also requires few tools. In the past, nearly every village boasted at least a few carvers among its habitants. Several traditional weather-vane motifs were thus created by these imaginative and skilled craftsmen. The most interesting aspect of this technique is that it always yields new and unique creations. Every rooster (Nos. 79 and 95) and every fish (Nos. 44 and 49) is different from all the others. As a result, some of the most unusual and striking weather vanes are hand-carved.

Figure 8. Weather vanes sold by Canadian Tire.

Hammering is a more complex technique. First, two sheets of fairly malleable metal, usually copper or tin, are cut according to a pattern and hammered onto pieces of hardwood carved in the same shapes. The two metal-covered pieces, which make up the two halves of the desired design, are then riveted, lap-jointed or soldered together to form a three-dimensional object (No. 8). Small parts, such as a rooster's bill, head or feet, are often fashioned of cast or wrought iron and soldered to the body. Similarly, fins are sometimes cut from sheet metal and soldered to the body of the fish.

The head or limbs may be weighted to balance the weather vane on its spindle.

Repoussé, a highly sophisticated form of hammering, is rarely found in Canadian weather vanes. The artisan hammers out a freehand design without using a form (No. 12). This technique is used mainly for weather vanes on monuments.

Cast iron was used mainly in commercially manufactured weather vanes. Most of the moulds were created by well-known craftsmen, who were still needed to perfect the work,

make any necessary changes and apply finishing touches. Not surprisingly, some manufacturers attempted to make use of the hydraulic press; however, they were apparently unsuccessful.

Carved weather vanes are often made of wood, whereas cut weather vanes are made of wood or metal. The most popular metal for hammered weather vanes is copper because of its high resistance to cracking and corrosion; and because of its malleability, it is ideally suited for intricate designs. Tin is also popular. In the past, weather vanes were covered with gold leaf or painted gold to make them shine in the sun. In the twentieth century, with the collapse of the weather-vane industry in the United States, gilding has been replaced by patina. Over the past few decades, the trend toward the "antique look" has given a new market value to weather vanes, which might otherwise have become commercially obsolete.

Unfortunately, most of the craftsmen of these marvellous objects remain unknown. However, the commercial manufacturers of weather vanes are fairly well-known through their catalogues. In Canada, the industry was negligible, and most factory-made weather vanes were ordered from the United States.

How Weather Vanes Work

In mechanical terms, a weather vane is a two- or three- dimensional figure mounted on a spindle. For the weather vane to work accurately, the figure must be off-centre of the spindle but properly balanced (No. 48: the body of the swordfish is located almost entirely on one side of the spindle). Wind blowing on the weather vane exerts more force on the side of the spindle with the larger surface, causing the figure to rotate. When the figure finally stops rotating, its smaller surface is windward.

It is usually the front of the figure that points into the wind. This is not always the case, however, depending on the artisan's ineptness or sense of humour. The pig in weather vane No. 37 for example, surely presented its backside to the wind as the spindle is located immediately in front of the hind legs.

To be properly balanced and thus function accurately, the weather vane must also be equally weighted on both sides of the spindle; otherwise, it will not turn with the wind. Artisans have resorted to a variety of techniques to balance the weight: adding a few drops of lead to the front of the figure; fashioning small parts, such as the head or limbs, from cast iron; and increasing the weight of some parts and making others lighter. Typical of the trial-and-error method of balancing is weather vane No. 15: The craftsman had to balance the weight of the horseman with an enormous pinion made of a double row of boards; a few holes were drilled in the small pinion in order to achieve the proper balance.

Motifs

Mainly through their motifs, weather vanes express various aspects of a culture. The most popular figures are positive symbols. For instance, the rabbit, a scourge to gardeners, is rarely represented; nor is the dog, whose symbolism is ambivalent. One common motif, however, is the beaver, whose industriousness, frugality, thriftiness and farsightedness were highly valued qualities in the Victorian era.

Needless to say, the rooster occupies a privileged position. Over one third of the entire collection consists of weathercocks, from steeples, wayside crosses, barns and houses. Horses, beasts of burden and of recreation, make up nearly twenty percent of the collection. The cow, the fish and the beaver each represent approximately ten percent. The rest of the collection consists of various other animals, a few heraldic motifs and abstract pieces, two boats and a lightning rod.

The sight of an animal silhouetted against the sky has often evoked a hunter's instinct. In fact, several weather vanes bear the scars of wounds inflicted by marksmen who were more interested in showing off their skill than in preserving heritage (No. 5). However, weather vanes do make tempting targets; they are relatively far away and clearly profiled in the sky and they constitute no risk for people or domestic animals. Moreover, they are a cooperative target — they move when they are hit and then immediately revert to their original position, as if inviting another shot.

Weather Vanes as Folk Art

Weather vanes are generally viewed with admiration and affection. Some are part of the religious world, such as the weathercocks on church steeples and wayside crosses. They are evidence of a venerable tradition and an expression of the imagination, practical genius and skill of the Canadian people. The art of handcrafting weather vanes died out in the late nineteenth century, and they subsequently became "art objects". Today, weather vanes are undeniably an integral part of folk art. Any contemporary study of folk art should automatically include at least a half-dozen weather vanes. Virtually all specialized magazines publish, from time to time, a short article on some aspect of weather vanes. Collectors and antique dealers marvel at their charm and evocative power while specialists analyse their practical and artistic qualities.

However, this was not always the case. In Canada, interest in weather vanes as folk art began only a few decades ago. Collectors and antique dealers were more aware than curators and museums of the artistic value of these objects, which served strictly practical purposes for most of their makers and owners. Until fairly recently, a startling number of pilferers roamed the countryside, scanning the horizon for weathercocks on house lanterns or wayside crosses or for any other type of weather vane on barn or shed rooftops. While the lure of profit was the motivation, it led to excesses such as forgery (No. 98) and even aggravated robbery. Whether fact or fiction, one story in the United States tells of a helicopter that swooped down and carried off a giant weather vane. Canada reports less spectacular thefts. However, some pilferers have boldly cut down wayside crosses with power saws in order to make off with weathercocks. Fortunately, not all collectors are of this bent. The discernment, determination and enthusiasm of serious collectors have made it possible to preserve a number of objects that bear witness to another era and a particular aesthetic sense. Moreover, thanks to the efforts of collector and antique dealers, the Canadian Museum of Civilization has acquired its weather vane collection. This explains, however, the lack of reliable documentation on the objects; the information provided is sometimes romanticized or even blatantly false. A typical example is the confusion surrounding weather vane No. 98, known as the Cap-Chat rooster.

Note:

The origins of most of the weather vanes are unverified. As they were acquired mainly from collectors and antique dealers the available documentation is not always complete or reliable.

The dimensions of the weather vanes are presented in descending order of size and are expressed in centimetres, rounded to the nearest half-centimetre.

Beavers

*H*onour to whom honour is due. The beaver is Canada's national emblem, symbolizing the industriousness and perseverance evinced by our ancestors in their struggle to adapt to the harsh Canadian climate. A bold architect, meticulous engineer and tireless builder, the beaver embodies the courage and ingenuousness of the pioneers who devised new shelters, clothes, foods, tools and games in order to overcome the isolation of the vast Canadian landscape and put down roots in the hard and hostile soil.

From an artistic perspective, the beaver's anatomy lends itself to amazing foreshortening and striking stylization.

1
Beaver
Saint-Martin, Quebec
Before 1957
Tin, iron, wood
142 x 58.5 x 58.5
A-539

This weather vane was probably commercially manufactured. Made of several tin pieces hammered and soldered together, the beaver is perched above the cardinal points and a globe.

2
Beaver
Pickering, Ontario
Early twentieth century
Sheet metal, iron
62 x 42 x 2.5
CCFCS 74-1267

Cut from a piece of sheet metal, this amusing beaver was a humorous silhouette against the skies of rural Ontario at the turn of the century.

3
Beaver
Quebec area
Late nineteenth century
Painted wood
81 x 80 x 2.5
CCFCS 74-280
Gift of B. McKendrie

4
Beaver
Quebec area
Late nineteenth century
Painted wood
82 x 80 x 2.5
CCFCS 74-335

Cut from pine board, these grumpy-looking beavers seem to point into the wind against their will.

5
Beaver

Quebec
Early nineteenth century
Sheet metal, iron, paint
108 x 70 x 5
CCFCS 73-613

Made of two galvanized iron sheets hammered and soldered together, this beaver was far too often the helpless victim of thoughtless young marksmen.

6
Beaver at Work

Omemee, Ontario
Late nineteenth century
Painted sheet tin, iron
80 x 39 x 4.5
CCFCS 79-1591. (P. & R. Price Coll.)

Composed of several moulded and soldered sheets of tin, this beaver is apparently busy stripping the trunk of a tree it has just felled.

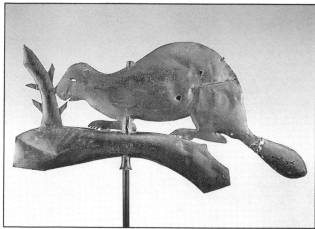

7
Beaver

Saint-Julie-de-Verchères, Quebec
Date unknown
Wood, iron
72.5 x 29.5 x 4
CCFCS 71-305

Cut from a pine board, this beaver is purportedly from a barn in Sainte-Julie-de-Verchères.

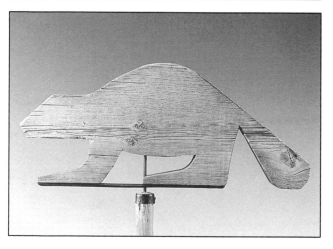

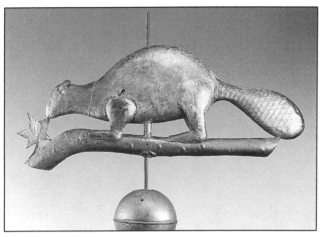

8
Beaver and Maple Leaf
L'Assomption, Quebec
Date unknown
Sheet tin, iron, wood
87 x 83 x 5.5
CCFCS 77-1045 (N. Sharpe Coll.)

Its powerful lines make this weather vane a true work of art. The original design incorporates Canada's two national symbols, the beaver and the maple leaf. Made up of several tin sheets hammered and soldered together, the beaver is perched above a copper sphere that represents the earth.

9
Beaver and Maple Leaves
South shore of lower St. Lawrence, Quebec
Date unknown
Sheet metal, iron, wood, paint
77 x 48 x 2
CCFCS 81-319 (N. Sharpe Coll.)

Cut from sheet metal and reinforced with wrought iron, this weather vane incorporates Canada's two national symbols, the beaver and the maple leaf. Its fine detail bespeaks the artisan's skill.

Horses

The French naturalist Buffon described the horse as the noblest conquest man has ever made. Compared with other domestic animals, the horse enjoys a closer relationship with humans, as partner and friend. It has provided us with speed, power and prestige. The horse has ploughed our fields, carried our loads, herded our animals, taken us to faraway lands, participated in our hunts and our wars, and played a key role in our games, races, jousts, tournaments and carousels.

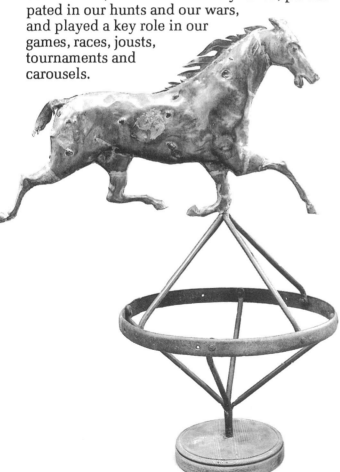

Whether a draught horse, a racehorse or a show animal, the horse is always a symbol of prestige and power, embodying fiery strength, eternal youth, virility and indomitability.

Thus, through the ages, the horse has been venerated, adulated, cherished and idolized. Alexander the Great erected an entire city around the tomb of his beloved horse Bucephalus. Caligula honoured his horse Incitatus with the rank of consul. A statue commemorates Cortez's El Morzillo, and Wellington's Copenhagen was buried with military honours.

Equine anatomy, particularly its sturdy and supple muscle structure, has always fascinated painters and sculptors of all schools and allegiances. Artisans in Canada, where the horse was once essential for survival, have represented it in a wide variety of artistic creations. The horse motif appears fairly frequently in Canadian weather vanes.

10
Ethan Allen
Richmond, Quebec
Date unknown
Copper, iron, wood
84 x 65.5 (base diam.)
CCFCS 71-312
Gift of L. Vary

With its slightly bowed head and its open muzzle, this horse also resembles the extremely popular Ethan Allen horse of the United States. It was probably commercially manufactured. Yet, the powerful design is evidence of artistic genius. The unusual shape of the spindle underscores the motion of the animal.

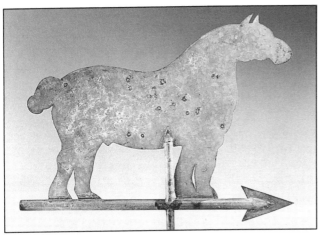

11
Horse on Arrow

Alberta
Date unknown
Sheet metal, iron
91 x 71 x 3
CCFCS 73-30

Cut from galvanized iron and mounted on a tubular steel arrow, this powerful draught horse was probably an Alberta farmer's favourite animal. Unlike the racehorse, the draught horse is not a common motif in Canadian weather vanes.

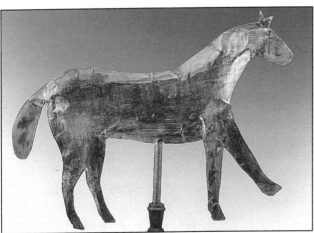

12
Horse

Varennes area, Quebec
Date unknown
Sheet tin, iron
91.5 x 64 x 9
CCFCS 71-307

Probably the work of an apprentice, this crudely fashioned horse consists of two tin sheets hammered and soldered together. It must have been a poor gauge of wind direction, as it is mounted dead centre on its spindle.

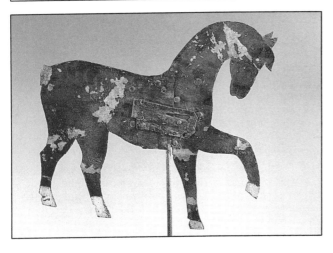

13
Horse

Martins River area, Nova Scotia
Date unknown
Sheet tin, iron, paint
44 x 41 x 1
CCFCS 74-1081

This elegant show horse has lost its stand. An antique dealer was interested in the figure's artistic value.

14
Horse

Annapolis Valley, Nova Scotia
Date unknown
Sheet metal, wood, iron, paint
89.5 x 26 x 1.5
CCFCS 81-35 (G. Ferguson Coll.)

The galloping horse on an arrow is a popular motif in Canadian weather vanes. Here, the motion of the horse is in striking contrast to the heaviness of the arrow. This horse bears an obvious resemblance to the one in weather vane No. 24. It is cut from sheet metal and mounted on a wooden arrow. The arrow's pointer and feather are also fashioned from sheet metal.

15
Horseman on Pinion

By George Ales
Wilmot Centre, Ontario
1910
Wood, metal, paint
69 x 33 x 5
CCFCS 76-490.1

The craftsman had to balance the weight of this horseman with an enormous pinion at the back. Holes were drilled in the smaller, front pinion, probably to achieve the proper balance.

16
Horse Harnessed to a Sulky

Richelieu area, Quebec
Date unknown
Sheet metal, iron, aluminum, paint
122 x 83 x 22.5
CCFCS 71-303
Gift of L. Vary

Although the horse harnessed to a sulky is a popular motif in American weather vanes, it is rarely found in Canada. This weather vane, which once stood atop a shed in the Richelieu area, was probably based on a catalogue illustration.

17
Horse
Verchères area, Quebec
Date unknown
Sheet steel, iron, paint
99 x 87.5 x 7
CCFCS 71-302

A blowtorch was probably used to cut this horse from thick plate steel, which is reinforced with metal rods.

18
Trotting Horse
Varennes area, Quebec
Date unknown
Sheet metal, iron, wood
61 x 46 x 3.5
CCFCS 71-313
Gift of L. Vary

This rough-hewn horse is also a poor gauge of wind direction, as the spindle is located dead centre.

19
Horse

Perth area, Ontario
Date unknown
Sheet metal, iron, wood, paint
74.5 x 61 x 1.5
CCFCS 71-52

This horse was cut from thick sheet metal with a blow-torch.

20
Trotting Horse

Martins River, Nova Scotia
Date unknown
Sheet metal, iron, paint
80 x 59 x 2
CCFCS 74-1082

This elegant trotting horse, cut with a blowtorch from thick sheet metal, clearly displayed to passers-by the householder's love of horses.

21
Ethan Allen

Irena, Ontario
Late nineteenth century
Sheet tin, iron, paint
133.5 x 119 x 37
CCFCS 79-1590 (P. & R. Price Coll.)

Carved from sheet tin and reinforced with wrought iron, this magnificent trotting horse resembles the famous Ethan Allen horse, a popular motif in American manufactured weather vanes. The tin base, an octagonal pyramid topped by a globe, is reminiscent of the finial used to protect a weak section of roof.

22
Trotting Horse

Saint-Paul-de-l'Île-aux-Noix, Quebec
Late nineteenth century
Sheet tin, iron, wood, paint
79 x 79 x 23
CCFCS 77-508

This magnificent and remarkably elegant racehorse is cut from sheet tin and reinforced with wrought iron. Expertly balanced on its spindle at the level of its forelegs, it must have been an extremely accurate gauge of wind direction.

23
Horse with Maple Leaf

Pictou, Nova Scotia
Late nineteenth century
Sheet metal, iron
106 x 102 x 9
CCFCS 78-560

Originally, this weather vane consisted of only the horse, made of two hammered and soldered metal sheets. The tube supporting a copper ball and a maple leaf cut from sheet metal was probably a later addition.

24
Horse

Pictou, Nova Scotia
Nineteenth century
Wood, iron, paint
136 x 89 x 89
CCFCS 78-559

This spirited horse testifies to the artistic talent of its unknown craftsman, who carved it from a single piece of wood in the last century. It bears certain similarities to weather vane No. 21.

25
Horseman

Fredericton, New Brunswick
Early twentieth century
Sheet metal, iron, wood
55 x 42 x 7
CCFCS 78-196 (P. & R. Price Coll.)

The horseman is not a common motif in Canadian weather vanes. Cut from two separate sheets of metal, horse and rider are riveted and soldered together. The slender head and limbs of the horse are reminiscent of the Lascaux cave paintings.

26
Horseman on Arrow

Nova Scotia
Circa 1950
Wood, iron, leather, paint
75 x 68 x 4
CCFCS 82-271 (P. & R. Price Coll.)

Cut and carved from one board, this weather vane incorporates two motifs — the horseman and the arrow.

Cows

*A*universal symbol of fertility and wealth, the cow is one of the world's most respected domestic animals. It is considered sacred in modern India, as it was in Pharaonic Egypt. In the Western world, cows are a valuable component of the economy. As milk producers, they symbolize the nourishing earth.

The bull symbolizes impetuosity, virility, blind passion and brute force. Formerly, bulls that could be tamed were put to work in the fields. Today, they are used mainly to inseminate the herd and ensure its continuity.

In Canada, particularly in the eastern part of the country, many dairy farms make a sometimes ostentatious show of their prosperity. Until fairly recently, weather vanes on barns were a practical way of advertising the type of livestock that the farmer raised. Today, standard commercial signs at farm gates depict the stylized profile of a cow in a pasture. Weather vanes with bull or cow motifs are, of course, most prevalent in thriving cattle-farming districts.

27
Cow
Knowlton, Quebec
Date unknown
Iron, metal, wood, paint
86 x 54 x 23
CCFCS 71-306

This cast-iron cow, spray-painted in gold, is obviously commercially manufactured.

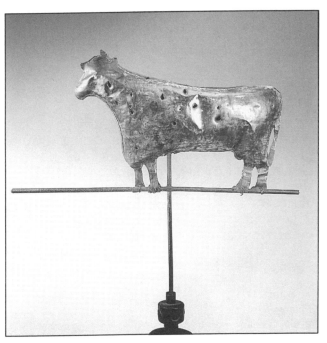

28
Bull

Sainte-Julie-de-Verchères, Quebec
Date unknown
Sheet metal, iron, wood, paint
116 x 86 x 11
CCFCS 71-301

Cut from two metal sheets, then hammered and welded together, this powerful bull was no doubt a dairy farm sign as well as a gauge of wind direction. Unfortunately, it was the frequent target of thoughtless marksmen.

29
Bull

Perth area, Ontario
Date unknown
Sheet metal, iron, paint
63 x 44 x 2.5
CCFCS 71-53

This clumsy bull with threatening horns is made of two metal sheets hammered, riveted and soldered together. Although of unknown origin, it was perhaps a sign on an Ontario dairy farm. Mounted dead centre on its spindle, it must have been useless as an indicator of wind direction.

30
Cow
Boucherville, Quebec
Date unknown
Sheet tin, iron, wood
95 x 60 x 8
CCFCS 71-311

This cow was probably used as a sign in a prosperous
dairy-farming area of Quebec.

31
Cow
Verchères area, Quebec
Date unknown
Sheet metal, copper, iron, wood, paint
96 x 64 x 19
CCFCS 77-535

Cut from two metal sheets, then flat-soldered together,
this cow was probably used as a sign on a dairy farm in
the Verchères area. The copper sphere on top is rarely
found in traditional weather vanes.

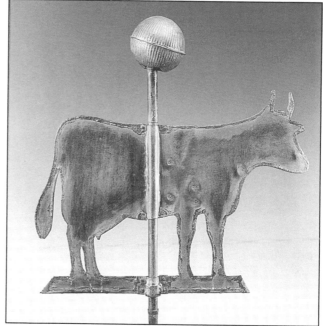

32
Cow

Verchères area, Quebec
Date unknown
Sheet metal, iron, wood, paint
80 x 78 x 19
CCFCS 71-304

This cow was cut from corrugated iron with a blowtorch.

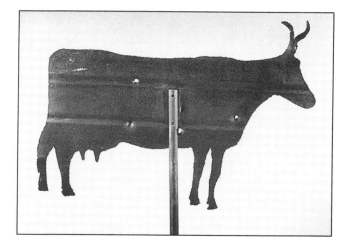

33
Cow

By Napoléon Birtz
Saint-Simon-de-Bagot, Quebec
1942
Sheet metal, iron, paint
91 x 46 x 3
CCFCS 75-926

This cow, cut from thick sheet metal with a blowtorch, was signed by the craftsman. On the left, the inscription reads: "Napoléon Birtz", and on the right: "1942/St. Simon".

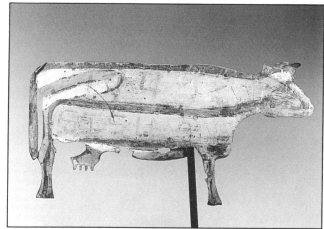

34
Cow

Port Perry area, Ontario
Date unknown
Wood, iron, paint
48 x 27.5 x 2
CCFCS 75-927 (P. & R. Price Coll.)

Cut and carved from a board, this stately ochre cow with white markings must have attracted the attention of passers-by with its striking silhouette against the Ontario sky.

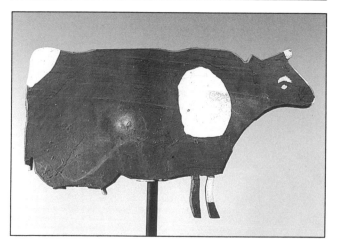

35
Cow
Alberta
Date unknown
Sheet steel, iron
83 x 72.5 x 4
CCFCS 73-29

In all likelihood, a blowtorch was used to cut this cow
from plate steel. It is mounted on a metal arrow.

36
Cow
Oshawa, Ontario
Circa 1914
Tin, iron, wood, paint
106.5 x 45.5 x 20.5
A-1326 A

This cow, cut from two tin sheets, was commercially
manufactured. It corresponds to No. 6444, on page 69
of *The Pedlar People Limited* catalogue (see Fig 7, p. 9).

Pigs

*I*n Western civilizations, pigs have a purely negative symbolism. They are associated with gluttony, selfishness, lewdness, baseness and perversity. However, they also have a high economic value. Their meat is appreciated, and they can be bred rapidly and cheaply. Shortly after the Second World War, many modern new pig farms sprang up, particularly in Eastern Canada. The following three weather vanes were probably used as signs on fairly prosperous pig farms.

37
Pig
Tessier family
Saint-Antoine-sur-Richelieu, Quebec
1942
Wood, iron, paint
75.5 x 66.5 x 7
CCFCS 78-447

Because of the close location of this pig's hind legs to the spindle, the animal's backside must have been windward. This is no doubt an intentionally humorous design.

38
Pig
Quebec
Date unknown
Sheet steel, iron, paint
94 x 48 x 4
CCFCS 83-972 (N. Sharpe Coll.)

Cut from plate steel with a blowtorch, this pig probably did double duty as the sign on a pig farm and as an efficient weather vane.

39
Sow
Harrowsmith, Ontario
Circa 1870
Sheet tin, iron
68 x 60 x 2.5
CCFCS 76-469

This magnificent, nineteenth-century sow conveys abundance and prosperity. Cut from a tin sheet, it was probably the sign on a flourishing pig farm. However, with the spindle located too close to its centre, it cannot have been an accurate indicator of wind direction.

Fish

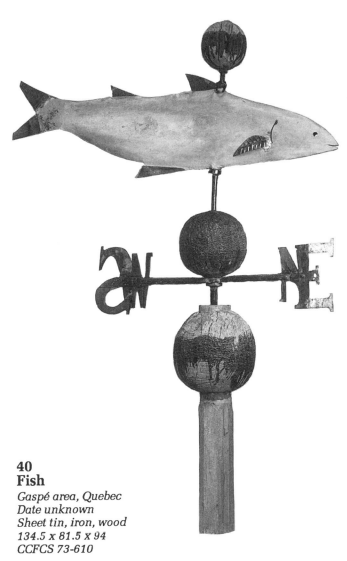

Weather vanes with a fish motif are found mainly in the Maritimes or the riverside villages of Quebec. The fish is, of course, the most apt weather-vane motif for people whose livelihood depends on the sea. Silhouetted against the sky and turning in the slightest breeze, it enables fishermen to forecast the weather and decide whether to set out to sea. Moreover, the fish weather vane advises passers-by that the householder is a fisherman or fish merchant.

The clean simple lines of the fish make it easy to cut and carve and help it withstand intemperate weather better than other, more complex designs. Its long, slim shape is particularly sensitive to the wind and allows it to be easily balanced. These two factors are essential to the proper functioning of a weather vane.

Finally, the fish is a universal symbol of life and fertility and has come to represent Christ himself to Christians. The Greek word *Ichthus* (fish) is the acrostic of *Iēsous Christos Theos HUios, Sōtēr* (Jesus Christ, Son of God, Saviour). As a result, the fish is prevalent in Christian symbology. In Canadian folk art, fish motifs appear mainly on sugar moulds and weather vanes.

40
Fish
Gaspé area, Quebec
Date unknown
Sheet tin, iron, wood
134.5 x 81.5 x 94
CCFCS 73-610

This lovely tin salmon is mounted on the four cardinal points and between two wooden spheres. Although this weather vane is believed to be from the Gaspé area, it was discovered in an Ontario antique shop.

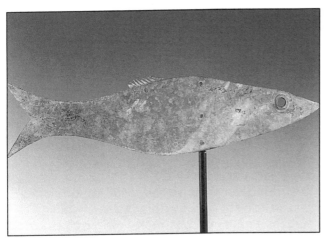

41
Fish

Madoc area, Ontario
Late nineteenth century
Sheet metal, iron, paint
76 x 54 x 18
CCFCS 78-438

This stylized fish is made of two galvanized iron sheets hammered and soldered together. In addition to being an accurate gauge of wind direction, it was perhaps a fish merchant's sign.

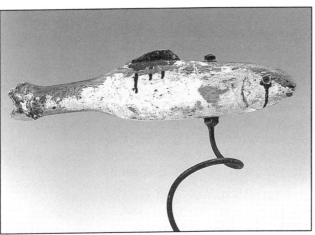

42
Fish

Maritimes
Date unknown
Pine, iron, paint
48 x 45 x 18
CCFCS 73-582

This lovely fish was carved from a single piece of pine.

43
Fish

Sainte-Marie, Beauce, Quebec
Date unknown
Sheet metal, iron, wood
55 x 42 x 4.5
CCFCS 71-322

Found in a shed in Sainte-Marie in Beauce, this fish weather vane is made of two metal sheets hammered, riveted and soldered together.

44
Fish
Sainte-Élizabeth, Quebec
Date unknown
Wood, iron
30.5 x 30 x 4.5
CCFCS 71-319

Carved from a single piece of pine, this fish was perhaps
a fish merchant's sign as well as a weather vane. It was
apparently found in Mr. Hermès Héneault's shed, in
Sainte-Élizabeth, near Joliette.

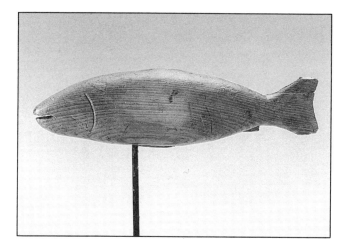

45
Fish
Bob Manary
Quyon, Quebec
Before 1961
Tin, iron
51 x 12 x 0.5
A-1114
Gift of Bob Manary

This fish was cut from sheet tin with shears.

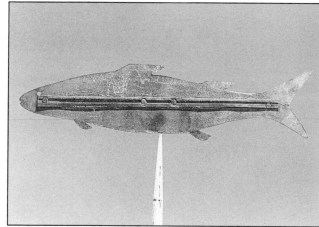

46
Fish
Léon Potvin
Baie Saint-Paul, Quebec
Before 1962
Wood
87.5 x 19.5 x 2
A-1675

This lovely fish, cut and carved from one board, served
perhaps as a sign for a riverside fish merchant.

47
Trout

By M. Duranceau,
La Prairie, Quebec
Date unknown
Copper, glass, iron, wood, paint
68.5 x 30 x 30
CCFCS 77-945 (N. Sharpe Coll.)

This glass-eyed, copper trout mounted on a ventilator cap
is apparently the work of a tinsmith who was an avid
trout fisherman. The design brings to mind the weather
vane's early links with the finial.

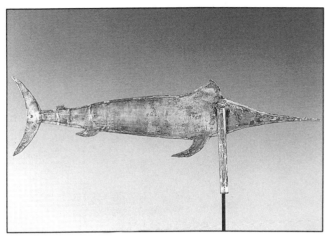

48
Swordfish

By Dollard Parent
Saint-Mathieu-du-Parc, Lac Bellemare, Quebec
1933
Sheet tin, iron, paint, varnish
83 x 30 x 2
CCFCS 71-768

Based on an illustration in *Popular Mechanics*, this sword-fish is evidence of the artistic talent and technical skill of its creator, who lap-jointed and soldered together two sheets from an old tin container.

49
Fish

New Brunswick
Early twentieth century
Pine, iron, paint
68.5 x 15 x 8.5
CCFCS 81-34 (G. Ferguson Coll.)

This marvellous fish was carved from a single piece of pine.

Various Animals

*T*his section features weather vanes with animal motifs that occur only once in the Museum's collection. These motifs are rarely found in Canadian weather vanes.

50
Frog
Cobourg area, Ontario
Early twentieth century
Sheet metal, iron, wood, asphalt shingles, rubber, paint
148 x 84 x 49
CCFCS 83-1825 (P. & R. Price Coll.)

This one-of-a-kind weather vane combines the four points of the compass with a frog and an arrow, all cut from thick sheet metal. It is mounted on a ventilator cap shaped like a rustic house.

51
Eagle
West Lake, Ontario
Nineteenth century
Sheet steel, iron
62 x 47 x 1.5
CCFCS 77-223 (P. & R. Price Coll.)

This highly stylized eagle must have cut a striking profile against the Ontario sky. It is made of pieces of plate steel, probably cut with a blowtorch and then soldered together. Unfortunately, it has lost one of its wings.

52
Peacock
White Cove, Nova Scotia
Early twentieth century
Wood, iron, paint
62 x 51 x 15
CCFCS 84-361 (P. & R. Price Coll.)

The ravages of time have not faded the remarkable elegance of this peacock, which was cut from one board. It was mounted on a carved wooden stand by an antique dealer.

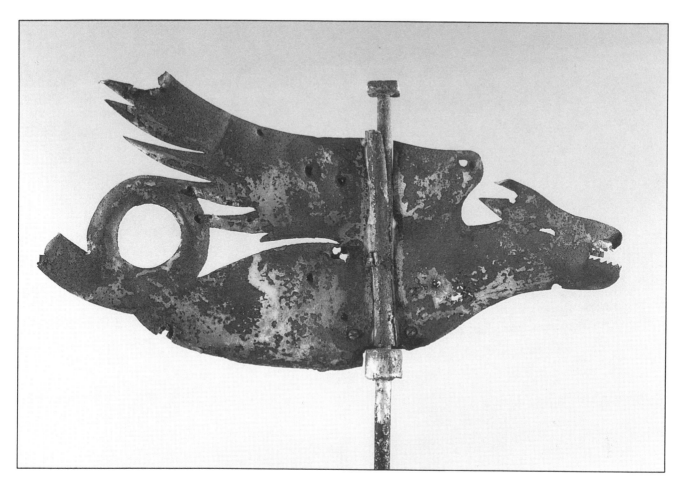

53
Dragon
Montréal, Quebec
Nineteenth century
Sheet tin, iron, wood
78 x 48 x 24
CCFCS 79-1592 (P. & R. Price Coll.)

This dragon was commercially manufactured, perhaps in
the United States. Made of two moulded tin sheets
soldered together, it was apparently discovered in the
Montréal area.

54
Squirrel
South shore of the lower St. Lawrence
Date unknown
Sheet metal, iron, paint
72.5 x 45 x 2
CCFCS 77-946 (N. Sharpe Coll.)

Cut from thick sheet metal with a blowtorch and
mounted on a wrought-iron arrow, this squirrel was a
striking silhouette against the Quebec sky.

Heraldic Motifs

*A*s explained in the introduction, noblemen of the Middle Ages customarily displayed banners with their coat of arms on the highest castle turret as a sign of their social status and allegiance. The heraldic tradition still lives on, as can be seen in some of the heraldic motifs in our weather-vane collection: a fleur-de-lis, a French flag and two banners of unknown symbolism.

55
Pennon
Lennoxville, Quebec
Date unknown
Sheet metal, copper, iron, wood, paint
195.5 x 71 x 71
CCFCS 73-614

The pennon of this weather vane was commercially manufactured and appeared as No. 19 in the A.B. & W.T. Westervelt catalogue. The cardinal points were also apparently factory-made, but their origin is unknown. This weather vane probably graced the roof of a house in Lennoxville, in the Eastern Townships. It is reminiscent of the pennons that topped the castles of noblemen in the Middle Ages.

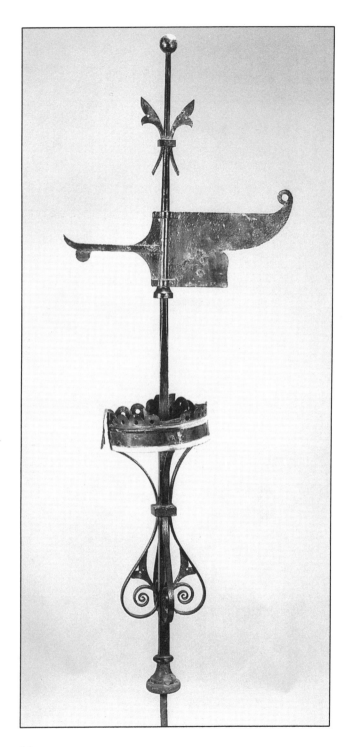

56
Pennon of Saint-Denis Club
Montréal, Quebec
Late nineteenth century
Wrought iron, paint
252 x 72 x 33
CCFCS 80-536
Gift of S. Raff

The two main components of this highly complex weather vane are a crown and a pennon, the heraldic meaning of which is unknown. It was installed on the rooftop of Montréal's Saint-Denis Club, which was built in 1850 and demolished in 1950.

57
Arrow
Annapolis Valley, Nova Scotia
Date unknown
Wood, iron, paint
117 x 12 x 6
CCFCS 81-36 (G. Ferguson Coll.)

Carved from a pine board, this arrow with its feather
shaped like a fleur-de-lis is an early example of the shift
toward artistic expression in weather vanes.

58
French Flag on Arrow
Baie-Saint-Paul area, Quebec
Date unknown
Sheet metal, iron, wood, paint
107 x 80 x 14
CCFCS 80-138 (N. Sharpe Coll.)

The unique design of this weather vane combines two
popular motifs — the arrow and the banner. The arrow is
made of metal sheets folded and soldered together. The
spindle location, close to the front, certainly ensured the
weather vane's reliable functioning.

Boats

*A*lthough the boat motif is popular in Maritime folk art, it is rarely found in weather vanes. Our collection includes only two such boats, a sloop and a steamship.

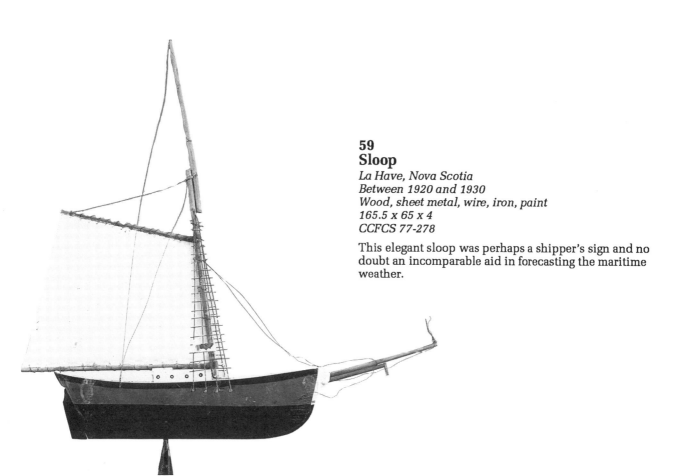

59
Sloop
La Have, Nova Scotia
Between 1920 and 1930
Wood, sheet metal, wire, iron, paint
165.5 x 65 x 4
CCFCS 77-278

This elegant sloop was perhaps a shipper's sign and no doubt an incomparable aid in forecasting the maritime weather.

60
Steamship
By Randall Smith
Ingomar, Nova Scotia
Between 1970 and 1976
Wood, plastic, wire, string, paint
150 x 53 x 5
CCFCS 77-311

This painted wood weather vane represents a steamship.
The extreme off-centre position of the boat on its spindle
made it an accurate gauge of wind direction.

Lightning Rods

*T*his section describes weather vanes mounted on top of lightning rods. Commercially manufactured in a fairly standard and easily recognizable style, they became popular in the 1920s.

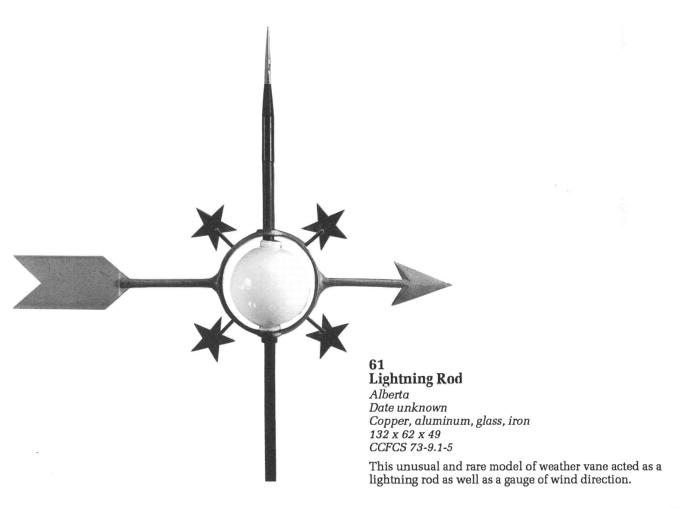

61
Lightning Rod
Alberta
Date unknown
Copper, aluminum, glass, iron
132 x 62 x 49
CCFCS 73-9.1-5

This unusual and rare model of weather vane acted as a lightning rod as well as a gauge of wind direction.

62
Horse on Arrow

L'Épiphanie, Quebec
Date unknown
Copper, iron, wood
62 x 56.5 x 12
CCFCS 71-315

This horse is made of two copper sheets hammered and lap-jointed together. Its position at the back of the cast-iron arrow made it a reliable indicator of wind direction. The weather vane was mounted on a carved wooden pedestal by an antique dealer.

63
Horse on Arrow

Origin unknown
Date unknown
Sheet tin, iron, copper, glass, paint
74.5 x 65 x 29.5
CCFCS 73-611

Made of two tin sheets moulded and soldered together, this horse is mounted on a cast-iron arrow.

64
Trotting Horse on Arrow
L'Assomption, Quebec
Date unknown
Sheet metal, iron, wood
58.5 x 52.5 x 12
CCFCS 71-316
Gift of L. Vary

65
Trotting Horse on Arrow
Quebec
Date unknown
Sheet metal, iron
57 x 22.5 x 3
CCFCS 73-607

Probably commercially manufactured, each of these two weather vanes consists of a horse made of moulded sheet metal and mounted on a cast-iron arrow.

66
Horse on Arrow
Origin unknown
Date unknown
Sheet tin, iron, copper, glass, paint
154 x 74.5 x 56
CCFCS 73-612

Made of two tin sheets moulded and soldered together,
this painted white horse is mounted on a cast-iron arrow
painted blue.

67
Bull on Arrow
Saint-Jean-de-Matha, Quebec
Date unknown
Sheet metal, iron, wood, paint
58 x 54 x 12
CCFCS 71-317

Incorporating the motifs of the arrow and the bull, this
weather vane was apparently the sign on a dairy farm in
the Joliette area.

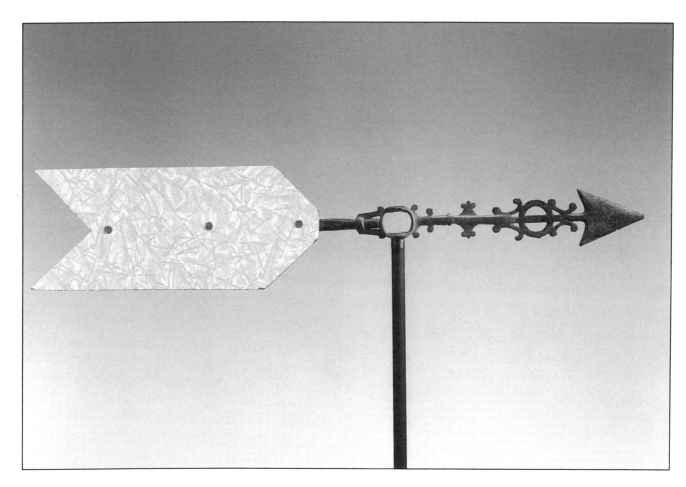

68
Arrow
Alberta
Date unknown
Iron, Arborite, copper
83 x 17.5 x 2.5
CCFCS 73-10

This cast-iron arrow with its Arborite feather is a recycled
object, which originally bore an animal at the rear, like the
preceding weather vanes.

Roosters

*T*he rooster is a universal symbol of the sun, as its crowing announces the approach of a new day. In ancient times, the rooster was revered for its intelligence and courage. From the depths of his misery, a wizened Job cried out: "Who...gives the cock its understanding?" (Job 38[39]:36). The rooster's vigilance and ardour won the admiration of the Greeks and Romans, who adopted it as their patron bird. Its noble bearing has made it a universal symbol of pride.

The early Christians made the rooster a symbol of their faith because of its role in Peter's denial of Christ. It came to symbolize vigilance, prayer and, in particular, the Resurrection of Christ and Redemption of all Christians. On early Christian sarcophagi and catacomb frescoes, Christ and Peter were often portrayed with a rooster at their feet or atop a column (Figs. 9 and 10).

The earliest example of a steeple cock is the ninth-century bronze rooster on the Brescia cathedral in the Piedmont region, in northern Italy. According to its Latin inscription, *gallum hunc fieri praecepit*, the cock was

69
Steeple Weathercock
Trois-Pistoles, Quebec
Date unknown
Sheet metal, wood, paint
83.5 x 57.5 x 21.5
CCFCS 73-529

This majestic rooster is made of several metal sheets hammered and soldered together. It was falsely claimed that it once graced the steeple of Sainte-Françoise church in Trois-Pistoles. An antique dealer mounted it on an elaborately carved ornament.

Figure 9. Sarcophagus in the Latran church, Rome.

Figure 10. Panel on the door of Saint Sabina Church, Rome.

produced on the order of Bishop Rambert in a.d. 820. One century later, the Bishop of Westminster erected a rooster on the steeple of his cathedral. The oldest representation of a steeple cock is on the famous Bayeux tapestry (1088–1092), which depicts, among other things, the 1065 erection of a steeple cock on Westminster Abbey. An old chronicle in Coutances also reports that in 1091 a hurricane destroyed part of the cathedral roof and blew away the steeple cock.

The custom of erecting a rooster on a church steeple thus dates as far back as medieval times. The tradition travelled with the early colonists to North America, as part of their religious and cultural heritage, and has remained particularly popular in Quebec.

Figure 11. Weathercock on Sacré-Coeur church, Hull, Quebec.

Figure 12. Wayside cross, Sainte-Marie, Quebec.

According to some sources, a steeple cock was erected on a parish church in Quebec's Outaouais region only once the debt for the building was totally paid off.

The rooster is a national as well as religious symbol. In addition to symbolizing Christian faith, it represents the French nation (Nos. 71, 83 and 86). The Gallic rooster is, in fact, a common sight in Francophone communities — on church steeples (Fig. 11), wayside crosses (Fig. 12), barn gables and rooftops of homes (Fig. 13).

Weathercocks on barns and farmhouses were usually carved by the farmer himself. Occasionally, he would rely on the skill of a neighbouring craftsman or the village tinsmith or blacksmith. The commercial

Figure 13. Cock on top of André Touchet's house, Aylmer, Quebec.

manufacturing of weather vanes became common in the eighteenth century, particularly in the United Sates, but steeple weathercocks continued to be handmade by rural craftsmen for many years.

The rooster's asymmetrical shape makes an ideal weather vane and is a source of artistic inspiration. Its broad tail feathers offer a large wind surface, causing the weathercock to rotate with the slightest breeze. It gauges wind direction both accurately and elegantly. In addition, its anatomy lends itself to flights of artistic fancy (Nos. 72 and 101) or to detailed naturalistic renderings (Nos. 91, 97 and 102).

Three Legends about the Rooster

One legend relates that Saint Peter, though contrite and penitent, harboured a deep grudge against roosters. He could not refrain from avenging himself on any rooster he encountered and even impaled those who were bold enough to crow in his presence. In his wrath, he made a point of displaying his victims in full view so as to discourage other roosters from such impudence. According to the legend, weathercocks became a familiar sight on church steeples from then on.

Another early Christian legend is about a rooster Mathias had killed to cook for Christ's last meal before his Ascension. Christ resurrected the bird, which flew off to announce its resurrection and that of Christ.

The third legend originates in the small village of Barcelos, in the Minho region of northern Portugal. In the village stands a fourteenth-century stone cross with a carved rooster at the feet of Christ. According to the legend, the villagers had been deeply upset by a crime committed by an unknown perpetrator. A Galician pilgrim on his way to Santiago de Compostela became the prime suspect and, despite his claims of innocence, was sentenced to be hanged. Before his execution, he asked to see the judge. His wish was granted, and he was brought before the judge, who was dining with a few friends. On the table was a roasted bird. To the general astonishment, the condemned man exclaimed, "As surely as I am innocent, this cock will crow if I am hanged." The company roared with laughter but did not dare touch the bird. The prisoner was led to the gallows. As the execution was about to take place, the roasted bird rose and began to crow. No one any longer doubted the Galician's innocence, and he was saved *in extremis* by the judge's prompt intervention. He resumed his pilgrimage to Santiago de Compostela. The Barcelos rooster has become a major theme in Portuguese folk art (Fig. 14).

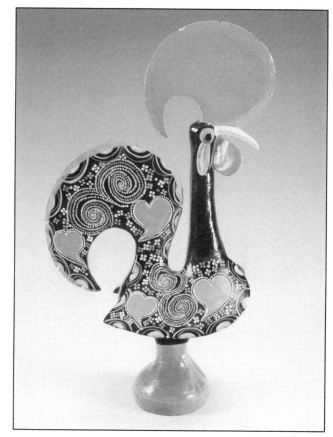

Figure 14. Barcelos rooster, painted plaster.

70
Steeple Weathercock
Saint-Guillaume-d'Upton, Quebec
Date unknown
Sheet metal, iron, wood, paint
122 x 69 x 17
CCFCS 73-528

This rooster is made of several pieces of sheet metal that have been cut, hammered and lap-jointed. It has been impossible to confirm whether this rooster actually did grace the Saint-Guillaume steeple.

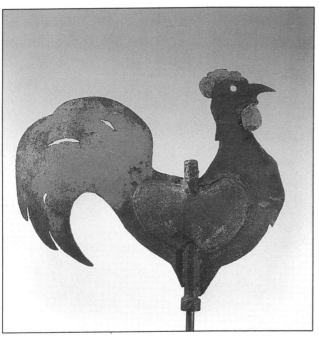

71
Steeple Weathercock
Saint-Élie-d'Orford, Quebec
Date unknown
Sheet steel, iron, wood, paint
80 x 52 x 4
CCFCS 73-530

Cut from a sheet of steel, probably with a blowtorch, this Gallic-looking rooster was a long-standing herald of vigilance atop the church steeple in Saint-Élie-d'Orford.

72
Steeple Weathercock

Louiseville, Quebec
Twentieth century
Sheet metal, tar, wood, paint
96 x 84 x 35
CCFCS 79-1587 (P. & R. Price Coll.)

This giant-tailed rooster is made of several pieces of sheet metal, hammered, tarred, soldered together and painted. Along with a second rooster, it apparently graced the twin-steepled church in Louiseville until 1976.

73
Steeple Weathercock

Sainte-Blandine, Quebec
Early nineteenth century
Wood, sheet metal, paint
64 x 63 x 19
CCFCS 71-309
Gift of L. Vary

Consisting of several pieces of cut and carved wood, this venerable patriarch has weathered the ravages of time, witnessing the passing of generations at the church of Sainte-Blandine, near Rimouski.

74
Steeple Weathercock
Île Bizard, Quebec
Date unknown
Sheet metal, iron, wood, paint
81.5 x 51 x 17.5
CCFCS 73-531.1

75
Steeple Weathercock
Île Bizard, Quebec
Date unknown
Sheet metal, iron, wood, paint
81.5 x 37 x 10.5
CCFCS 73-531.2

These look-alike roosters are made of several pieces of sheet metal hammered and soldered together. They apparently topped the twin-steepled church of Île Bizard, near Montréal.

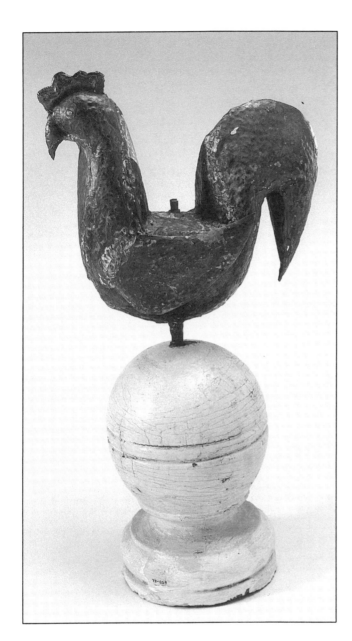

76
Weathercock on Wayside Cross
Trois-Rivières, Quebec
Nineteenth century
Copper, iron, wood
43.5 x 23.5 x 14
CCFCS 73-639

This sullen-looking rooster is made of several copper pieces hammered and soldered together.

77
Weathercock on Wayside Cross
Sainte-Mélanie, Quebec
Date unknown
Sheet tin, iron, wood, paint
70 x 46.5 x 11
CCFCS 71-310
Gift of L. Vary

Two tin sheets were moulded and soldered together to
fashion this aggressive-looking rooster, which apparently
decorated a wayside cross in Sainte-Mélanie, near Joliette.
It strongly resembles weather vane No. 80.

78
Weathercock on Wayside Cross
Saint-Barthélemy, Quebec
Date unknown
Sheet metal, iron, wood, paint
85 x 54 x 16
CCFCS 71-323

Several tin pieces were hammered and soldered together
to form this strong-limbed fighting cock, which graced Mr.
Lafontaine's wayside cross in Saint-Barthélemy.

79
Weathercock on Wayside Cross

Quebec
Date unknown
Wood, iron, paint
55 x 43 x 11.5
CCFCS 73-532

This medieval-looking rooster was carved from a single piece of wood.

80
Weathercock on Wayside Cross

Saint-Jude, Quebec
Date unknown
Sheet tin, iron, paint
52 x 48 x 8.5
CCFCS 71-314
Gift of L. Vary

Made of two tin sheets moulded and soldered together, this fighting cock apparently graced a wayside cross in Saint-Jude, near Saint-Hyacinthe. It is very similar to weather vane No. 78.

81
Weathercock on Wayside Cross
Saint-Ours, Quebec
Early twentieth century
Wood, sheet metal, iron, paint
72 x 49 x 14
CCFCS 77-943 (N. Sharpe Coll.)

The body of this magnificent rooster is of carved pine. The comb and the tail feathers were cut from sheet metal and screwed or nailed to the body.

82
Weathercock on Wayside Cross
Mr. Therrien
Saint-Denis-sur-Richelieu, Quebec
Date unknown
Sheet copper, iron, wood, paint
79 x 50 x 14.5
CCFCS 77-509

Consisting of several copper sheets hammered and soldered together, this rooster, stretching skyward, topped Mr. Therrien's wayside cross in Saint-Denis-sur-Richelieu.

83
Weathercock on Wayside Cross
Saint-Georges, Beauce, Quebec
Date unknown
Sheet steel, iron, paint
81 x 37.5 x 9
CCFCS 71-308
Gift of L. Vary

Cut from plate steel, probably with a blowtorch, this very
Gallic-looking rooster, perched proudly on a globe atop its
wayside cross, acted as a constant reminder of the need
for vigilance.

84
Weathercock on Wayside Cross
Saint-Félix-de-Valois, Quebec
Date unknown
Wood, iron, paint
53 x 33.5 x 25
CCFCS 71-318
Gift of L. Vary

Carved from a single piece of wood, this compact rooster
originally topped a wayside cross. An antique dealer
perched it on this unseemly carved wooden stand.

85
Weathercock on Wayside Cross

Jean Desrochers
Saint-Jacques, Montcalm, Quebec
Date unknown
Sheet metal, iron, paint
27 x 25 x 9
CCFCS 78-256.7 (N. Sharpe Coll.)

Several thin sheets of metal were hammered and soldered together to produce this small rooster, which decorated the wayside cross on the Desrochers family property in Saint-Jacques.

86
Chanticleer

Newmarket, Ontario
Late nineteenth century
Sheet metal, iron, paint
75 x 60.5 x 4
CCFCS 79-1589 (P. & R. Price Coll.)

Cut from thick sheet metal, this regal bird strikes the traditional pose of the Gallic rooster, with its puffed-up chest and flowing tail feathers.

87
Weathercock on Wayside Cross

Berthierville, Quebec
Date unknown
Sheet tin, iron, wood
43 x 34 x 12
CCFCS 71- 321

This fighting cock, which dominated a wayside cross in
the Berthierville area, was made by hammering and weld-
ing together two tin sheets.

88
Weathercock

By George Raithby
Dorchester, Ontario
Mid-nineteenth century
Wood, sheet tin, paint
97.5 x 74 x 3.5
CCFCS 79-1854 (P. & R. Price Coll.)

Cut from one board, this splendid tin-combed bird is
an expression of the craftsman's strong artistic sense.
Extremely simple techniques were employed to give a
distinctive character to the highly stylized design.

89
Weathercock

Quebec
Late nineteenth century
Sheet tin, wood, paint
107 x 70 x 35
CCFCS 79-1588 (P. & R. Price Coll.)

The rounded and stylized contours of this rooster convey
an impertinent energy. Cut from two tin sheets, then hammered and soldered together, it is painted a copper tone.

90
Weathercock
Farnham, Quebec
Date unknown
Wood, iron, paint
41 x 27 x 12
CCFCS 77-948 (N. Sharpe Coll.)

Carved from a single piece of pine, this lovely little rooster was one of a flock of birds perched in a tree in the garden of an anonymous but talented sculptor. Even the deplorable stand on which it is now mounted cannot detract from the artisan's strong aesthetic sense.

91
Chanticleer
Stormont, Ontario
Date unknown
Sheet tin, iron, wood, paint
58.5 x 44.5 x 40
CCFCS 80-111

Two tin sheets were hammered and soldered together to fashion this Gallic rooster, regally perched on a tiny globe of the earth atop the four cardinal points.

92
Weathercock
Drummondville area, Quebec
Date unknown
Wood, paint
47 x 36 x 12
CCFCS 75-936

Carved from a single piece of wood, this clumsy-looking barn cock is nevertheless original.

93
Weathercock

Quebec
Late eighteenth century
Wood, tin, iron
47 x 43 x 12
A-2690

This wizened bird is carved from a single piece of wood and covered with tin.

94
Weathercock

Quebec
Date unknown
Sheet tin, copper, iron, wood, paint
89 x 46 x 20
CCFCS 73-615

Cut from two tin sheets, then moulded and soldered together, this fighting cock perches regally on a globe, as though emitting a vibrant appeal for universal vigilance.

95
Weathercock

Saint-Casimir, Quebec
Date unknown
Wood, iron, paint
34 x 20 x 7
CCFCS 77-947 (N. Sharpe Coll.)

With its body carved from a single piece of wood and its grooved tail feathers, this rooster bespeaks the maker's artistic talent and technical skill.

96
Weathercock

Saint-Henri-de-Lévis, Quebec
Date unknown
Sheet tin, iron, wood
98 x 52.5 x 19
CCFCS 77-944 (N. Sharpe Coll.)

This highly stylized rooster, made of several tin sheets moulded and soldered together, is awkwardly balanced on a wooden globe. It apparently indicated wind direction from the rooftop of a barn in Saint-Henri-de-Lévis.

97
Chanticleer
Annapolis Valley, Nova Scotia
Late nineteenth century
Copper, iron, wood, paint
59 x 39 x 15
CCFCS 75-911

This fighting cock with its deadly spurs is made of two copper sheets moulded and soldered together. This motif is rarely found in Maritime weather vanes.

98
Chanticleer
Anonymous tinsmith
Longueuil, Quebec
Early 1970s
Copper, iron, wood
121 x 76.5 x 30
CCFCS 73-527

An antique dealer commissioned a talented Longueuil tinsmith to produce this majestic cock, which was falsely attributed to the Cap-Chat church in the Gaspé. It consists of several copper pieces cut, hammered, riveted and welded together, and has apparently been coated with artificial patina.

99
Weathercock
North York, Ontario
Mid-nineteenth century
Sheet steel, iron
67 x 31 x 0.5
CCFCS 74-735

Cut from plate steel, this tiny rooster appears to strut with its tail fanned out like a peacock's. The sharp contrast between its arrogant pose and its small size makes the bird quite humorous.

100
Weathercock
Annapolis Valley, Nova Scotia
Date unknown
Sheet metal, iron, wood, paint
51 x 46 x 46
CCFCS 78-331

Cut from two metal sheets, then hammered and soldered together, this fleshy-looking cock surmounts the four cardinal points. The rooster motif is rare in Maritime weather vanes.

101
Weathercock

Trépannier family,
Saint-Adelphe, Quebec
Date unknown
Copper, iron, wood, paint
82 x 57 x 22
CCFCS 77-503

This splendid bird is made of several copper pieces
hammered and soldered together. Its stylized contours
are highly evocative, and its powerful tail surely made
it an excellent weather vane. It is perched on a globe,
symbolizing the earth.

102
Chanticleer

Origin unknown
Date unknown
Sheet metal, paint
48 x 46 x 0.5
CCFCS 75-1038

This stately Gallic rooster was cut from a metal oil barrel
with the trade name "Gargoyle/Mobiloil/York". It is a
striking example of recycling by past generations.

103
Weathercock
Chambly area, Quebec
Before 1924
Tin, iron, wood
98 x 65 x 14
A-1807

This surly-looking rooster, made of several hammered and soldered tin sheets, was acquired for the Museum by Marius Barbeau in 1924. On loan to the Musée régional de Chambly, it was returned to the Museum in May 1965.

104
Weatherclock
L'Ange Gardien, Quebec
Circa 1920
Copper, iron
90 x 63.5 x 63.5
A-2202

This bellicose-looking rooster is made of copper pieces hammered and soldered together. It resembles medieval cocks in that it has no feet.

Conclusion

In their own way, weather vanes reflect their
creators' struggles and hopes, and the cultural
interests of the institutions that preserve them.
They recall the hardships of our ancestors,
whose survival in this land depended largely
on their knowledge of the winds. Weather
vanes are also a reminder that humans do not
live on bread alone, but are sustained by the
beauty of artistic creation.

Bibliography

[Anonymous]. 1945. "Washington's Weather Vane." *Antiques* XLVII, 2: 105.

[Anonymous]. 1954. *Catalogue of Weathervanes.* New York: Associated American Artists Galleries.

A.B. and W.T. Westervelt. 1982. *American Antique Weather Vanes. The Complete Illustrated Westervelt Catalog of 1883.* New York: Dover Publications Inc.

Allen, Edward B. 1925. "Old American Weathervanes: Artistic Charm of the Few Surviving Vanes by Craftsmen of Colonial and Revolutionary Times." *International Studio* XXX: 450-453.

———. 1954. "The Useful and Agreeable." *Time* (Sept. 27): 80.

———. 1964. "Vanes." *The New Yorker* (Sept. 12): 39–40.

Arendt, Ch. 1886. *La signification du coq sur les clochers de nos églises.* Collection L'organe de l'art chrétien. Luxembourg.

Ayrton, O. Maxwell. 1903. "Some Modern Weathervanes." *International Studio* XIX, 3: 131.

Barraud, l'Abbé. 1850. "Recherches sur les coqs des églises." *Bulletin monumental de la Société française d'archéologie* II, vi: 277–290.

Bishop, Robert, and Patricia Coblenz. 1981. *A Gallery of American Weathervanes and Whirligigs.* New York: E.P. Dutton and & Co.

Bouet, G. 1849. "De l'ancienneté des coqs sur les tours d'églises." *Bulletin monumental de la Société française d'archéologie* II, v: 532–533.

Buckert, Isle, and Alexander Nesbitt. 1970. *Weathervanes and Weathercreatures.* Newport, R.I.: Third and Elm Press.

Cancellieri. 1786. "Cur veteres Christiani turribus campanariis gallos imponerent." *De secretariis basilicae vaticanae* III: 1363–1389.

Chamberlain, S. 1932. "Le Coq Gaulois Comes Down from Its Perch." *American Architect* CXLII: 14–16.

Christensen, Erwin O. 1951. "Weathervanes." *Antiques* III: 198–200.

Crosnier, Augustin Joseph. 1859. "Dernier mot sur le coq superposé à la Croix." *Bulletin monumental de la Société française d'archéologie* III, v: 577–596.

Decorde, Jean-Eugène. 1857. *Le coq des clochers.* Neufchâtel-en-Braye: E. Duval.

E.G. Washburne and Co. 1920. *Catalogue of Copper Silhouette Vanes.* New York: [E.G. Washburne and Co.].

Eberlein, Harold Donaldson. 1912. "Weather-Vanes." *American Homes and Gardens* IX: 392–394, 403.

Eymery, Alexis Blaise. 1815. *Dictionnaire des girouettes: ou Nos contemporains peints d'après eux-mêmes.* 2nd ed. Paris: A. Eymery.

Fitzgerald, Ken. 1967. *Weathervanes and Whirligigs.* New York: Clarkson N. Potter.

Gardner, John Starkie. 1911. *English Ironwork of the Seventeenth and Eighteenth Centuries: An Historical and Analytical Account of the Development of Exterior Smithcraft*, 300–320. London: B.T. Batsford.

Holland, Muriel. 1965. "Something in the Air." *Coming Events in Britain* (Dec.): 24–26.

J.W. Fiske. 1883. *Illustrated Catalogue and Price List of Copper Weather Vanes and Finials Manufactured by J.W. Fiske.* New York: [J.W. Fiske].

——. 1971. *J.W. FISKE 1893. Copper Weathervanes, Bannerets, Lightning Rods, Stable Fixtures. Illustrated Catalog and Historical Introduction.* American Historical Catalog Collection. Princeton: The Pyne Press.

Jenkins, Dorothy H. 1968. "Weathervanes." *Woman's Day* (July): 85–86.

Kaye, Myrna. 1966. "Hark: The Herald Angel." *Yankee* (Dec.): 42–44.

——. 1975. *Yankee Weathervanes.* New York: E.P. Dutton & Co., Inc.

Kelly, J.F. 1941. "Three Early Connecticut Weather-Vanes." *Old Time New England* XXXI, 4: 96–99.

Kenneth Lynch and Sons. 1971. *Weathervanes and Cupolas.* Canterbury, Conn.: Canterbury Publishing Co.

Klamkin, Charles. 1973. *Weathervanes: The History, Design, and Manufacture of an American Folk Art.* New York: Hawthorn Books Inc.

L.W. Cushing and Sons. 1883. *Weathervane Catalogue No. 9.* Waltham, Mass.: [L.W. Cushing and Sons].

Leclerq, Henri. 1914. "Coq." *Dictionnaire d'archéologie chrétienne et de liturgie* III, 2: 2886–2905.

Lipman, Jean. 1948. *American Folk Art in Wood, Metal and Stone*, 13–14, 49–72, 191. New York: Pantheon.

Lipman, Jean, and Alice Winchester. 1974. "Weathervanes and Whirligigs." In *The Flowering of American Folk Art, 1776-1876*, 138-151. The Whitney Museum of American Art. New York: Viking Press.

Macdonald, W.A. 1928. "The Man Who Tells the World Which Way the Wind Blows." *Boston Transcript*, Magazine Section (July 7) Pt. 5: 1–2.

Martin, Eugène. 1904. "Le coq du clocher. Essai d'archéologie et de symbolisme." *Mémoires de l'Académie Stanislas* I, 6: 1–40.

Miller, Steve. 1984. *The Art of the Weathervane.* Exton, Penn.: Schiffer Publishing Ltd.

Needham, Albert. 1953. *English Weathervanes: Their Stories and Legends from Medieval to Modern Times.* Haywards Heath, Sussex, U.K.: Charles Clark Ltd.

The Pedlar People Limited. 1912. *Pedlar Fireproofing Products. Catalogue No. 20R.* Oshawa: The Pedlar People Limited.

Romaine, Lawrence B. 1937. "Weathervanes." *The Chronicle of the Early American Industries Association* I, 21: 8.

Stoyle, Lewis E. 1931. "Vanes Fellows Always Found at Their Places of Business." *Boston Transcript* (Mar. 25) Pt. 3: 1.

———. 1931. "Turtles, Hares, Dogs and Geese Tell Which Way the Wind Blows." *Boston Transcript,* Travel Section (July 8): 1.

Swam, Mabel M. 1933. "On Weather Vanes." *Antiques* XXIII, 2: 64–65.

Thomas, John, and Betty Thomas. 1931. "Vanishing Vanes." *Sunday-Time Union* (Aug.): B-7.

Thwing, Leroy L. 1937. "Deacon Shem Drowne: Maker of Weathervanes." *The Chronicle of the Early American Industries Association* II, 1: 1–2, 7.

Van Court, Robert H. 1916. "New Type of the Weathervane." *American Magazine of Art* VII, 12: 489–493.

Wellman, Rita. 1939. "American Weathervanes." *House Beautiful* XXXI: 50–54, 69.

Whipple, J. Rayner. 1940. "Old New England Weather Vanes." *Old Time New England* XXXI, 2: 44–56.

Sources of Illustrations

Fig. 1   Courtesy of Mrs. K. Kuzyk, Winnipeg.

Fig. 2   Photograph by Harry Foster. Constructed according to a drawing by Stuart and Revett, taken from John Travlos, *Pictorial Dictionary of Ancient Athens* (New York: Praeger Publishers, 1971), 283-285.

Fig. 3   Photograph by Harry Foster.

Fig. 4   Courtesy of the Statens Historiska Museum, Stockholm, Sweden, SHM 150-23.

Fig. 5   Photograph by Harry Foster.

Fig. 6   Photograph by Harry Foster.

Fig. 7   Photograph by Harry Foster.

Fig. 8   Courtesy of Canadian Tire Corporation.

Fig. 9   Taken from Henri Leclercq, *Dictionnaire d'archéologie chrétienne et de liturgie*, III, 2, 1914, 2891–2892.

Fig. 10   Taken from Henri Leclercq, *Dictionnaire d'archéologie chrétienne et de liturgie*. III, 2, 1914, 2903–2904.

Fig. 11   Photograph by Harry Foster.

Fig. 12   Photograph by Marius Barbeau, 1919, NMC 45886.

Fig. 13   Photograph by Harry Foster.

Fig. 14   Photograph by Dennis Fletcher. This Barcelos rooster (CCFCS 76-1429) was acquired in Montréal in 1976 from Maria Amaral.

The weather vanes from the collection of the Museum were photographed by Dennis Fletcher and Harry Foster.